Pepper Persley

NOT TOO ANYTHING

Illustrated by
Jessica Jones

YOUNG
AUTHORS
PUBLISHING

Hi! My name is Pepper Persley, and I'm a reporter.

When I was little, I traveled with my dad to my very first New York Liberty's game. I was always interested in sports, so this was an exciting moment for me! After the game, I realized I had questions for the players.

We took a chance and sent the team an email. We originally thought they would send back answers through email, but they actually wanted me to interview a player, Sugar Rodgers, in person!

I had asked questions of several famous people like Chris Evans, Zoe Saldana, and Chadwick Boseman on the television show *Good Morning America*, so this was not my first time on camera. However, this was my very first time interviewing an athlete who was doing something I dreamed of doing! This moment would lead me to conduct interviews with other professional sports teams. Though my journey is exciting, it has not always been easy.

ADWEEK MOST POWERFUL WOMEN IN SPORTS

Many journalists know from a young age that they want to pursue a career in the field, but few act on those ambitions with as much conviction as Persley, an 11-year-old sports reporter and broadcaster whose professionalism and sideline poise have captivated audiences across social platforms and network television alike. This summer alone, she has hosted a Title IX panel for Nike, reported courtside for the WNBA Champion Las Vegas Aces and took over the Instagram of the WNBA's Seattle Storm.

Although she has a passion for basketball, Persley also knows her way around the baseball diamond, a skill set that allowed her to report live from the MLB Little League Classic for ESPN in August. Persley, who cites Serena Williams as a role model, has high expectations for the future of women's sports and even higher expectations for herself.

"Be yourself, and don't let anyone dim your shine," she said. -Mark Stenberg

In second grade, I was the only Black student in my class, and none of my really close friends were in my class either. So, I was happy when I met two girls who both seemed nice. The three of us all shared similar interests, too!

But I slowly noticed that they were starting to exclude me around other students and dismiss my passions, like my love for sports.

One day, the two girls shared that they were having a playdate and would bring me a present the following school day. But what I received from them, a letter, was quite the opposite.

In the letter, the girls said that I didn't share, was a copycat, and was negative. To them, I was "too bossy." What hurt the most was being called "too athletic."

How could I be too much of anything when I was simply being myself?

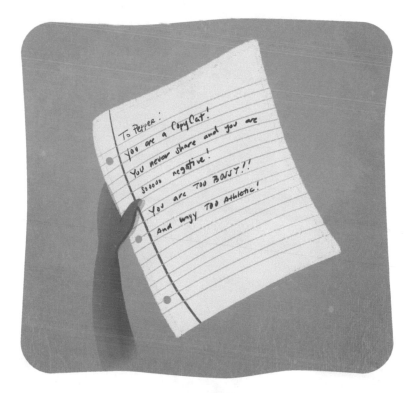

Despite their bullying, it was the beginning of my sports journalism career that helped me learn that, regardless of what others think of me, being my whole self is more than enough. And I wouldn't let their meanness stop me.

At the time of my first interview, I didn't have many of the mentors in sports journalism that I have now. I remember having a lot of questions about sports that my parents couldn't always answer. So, I turned to interviews.

Studying other interviews helped me prepare for my own conversations. I learned how to best prepare for interviews by researching the players, their interests, watching recent games, and researching their competitors.

I was 6 years old when I interviewed Sugar Rodgers. I don't remember being nervous, but I was definitely excited. I remember my parents cheering me on the whole time and me being comfortable in front of the camera.

After my interview with Sugar Rodgers, I was excited to continue growing my craft. I wanted to keep my interviews going to learn all I could about the WNBA players and their experiences, so I started emailing teams' PR and asking for opportunities.

New Message:

Hi!
My name is Pepper Persley and I'm interested in interviewing your sports team. Can we schedule some time to

Many times, teams would say yes to me doing interviews or going to press conferences. However, sometimes people assumed that, because of my age, I wasn't knowledgeable enough to be in the rooms or on calls to ask my questions.

Those were tough times for me—it made me feel like I didn't belong in those spaces simply because I was young. But I know that wasn't true.

I've never let my age stop me from pursuing what I love and what I'm good at.

I'd always loved basketball and had been playing for years, so I chose to focus on interviewing WNBA players to try to bring more attention to the league — I realized the WNBA didn't seem to have as many fans as the NBA, and as a fan myself, I couldn't understand why.

This only made me want to work harder to do the journalism work that I loved so I could help change that. Even now, I try to connect with all of the Black female sports reporters I know because it takes a real community to build big change.

My next big interview was with Diana Taurasi of the Phoenix Mercury, one the best players to ever play basketball. I remember knowing that she was an intense player, so I was a little nervous about my interview.

But I had nothing to be nervous about—she was really nice and we had an amazing conversation. She's someone I still have a connection with today!

During our chat, she gave me a great basketball drill to help improve my shooting. Thanks to my interview with her, I learned that players can very often be different on and off the court, and to keep an open mind when meeting and interviewing people for the first time.

Each of my interviews has opened new doors for me, and one of the most well-known people I've interviewed was former President George W. Bush.

I did the interview during my sideline reporting for the MLB Little League World Series KidsCast. The interview was great, and the former president was really nice with high energy! After the interview, he told me, "ESPN did a great job hiring you," which was such a confidence boost especially because I was interviewing a President in front of millions of people!

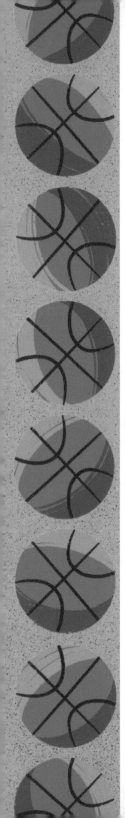

Natasha Cloud

Ali Krieger

Tina Charles

During this time, I was working on a project where successful professionals could share their bullying experiences and how they overcame the negativity.

I interviewed professional athletes such as former New York Liberty player Tina Charles, Natasha Cloud from the Washington Mystics, and Ali Krieger from the United States Women's National Soccer Team.

The advice from those people was some of the most impactful to me. In addition to their advice, it was so beneficial to know that these successful people had experienced something so similar to me.

My conversations with these female athletes taught me how valuable I am to any and all spaces. My dreams, too!

These interviews led to me creating and sharing an anti-bullying video called "Not 2 Athletic!"

To create the video, my dad and I put together a series of interviews that I conducted. The video included stories and advice from Olympians, WNBA players like Ariel Atkins and Reshanda Gray, members of the US Women's National Soccer Team including Ashlyn Harris and Ali Krieger, and even Liz Plank, an award-winning journalist!

I've received a lot of great advice, but the most meaningful piece of advice was to never change who I am because of what others say and to know that there are people who will support me for being me.

After releasing the "Not 2 Athletic" video, my passion for sharing stories continued to grow. So, during the COVID-19 pandemic, I started a podcast called "Dish With Pepper." On my podcast, I feature athletes, coaches, journalists, broadcasters, and others who inspire me.

DON'T STOP BELIEVING

Hosting my podcast and interviewing were dreams of mine. I encourage everyone to chase their dreams and believe in themselves, no matter how scary it may seem. I applied that lesson to my podcast because many kids aren't starting their careers at young ages like me, but I don't want kids to feel they have to wait to follow their dreams.

ON AIR

Since launching my podcast, I've worked with Nike, the National Women's Soccer League, the Women's Sports Foundation, and the Project Play Summit. I've become one of the youngest people to broadcast professional sport events for the NBA, WNBA, and MLB!

I've been profiled on television and conducted interviews on the 2022 American Music Awards red carpet with celebrities like P!nk, Kelly Rowland, Sabrina Carpenter, Sheryl Lee Ralph, and more.

I was even named one of the "Most Powerful Women in Sports" by *AdWeek* for all of my hard work!

ADWEEK MOST POWERFUL WOMEN IN SPORTS

Many journalists know from a young age that they want to pursue a career in the field, but few act on those ambitions with as much conviction as Persley, an 11-year-old sports reporter and broadcaster whose professionalism and sideline poise have captivated audiences across social platforms and network television alike. This summer alone, she has hosted a Title IX panel for Nike, reported courtside for the WNBA Champion Las Vegas Aces and took over the Instagram of the WNBA's Seattle Storm.

Although she has a passion for basketball, Persley also knows her way around the baseball diamond, a skill set that allowed her to report live from the MLB Little League Classic for ESPN in August. Persley, who cites Serena Williams as a role model, has high expectations for the future of women's sports and even higher expectations for herself.

"Be yourself, and don't let anyone dim your shine," she said. -Mark Stenberg

But I would not have achieved those wonderful moments without learning so much from all the women athletes who gave me a chance to ask questions and to learn from them.

Pepper, 6 yrs old with Sugar Rodgers! :)!

Ashlyn & Pepper ♥

Pepper with George W. Bush!

While I'm proud of what I've accomplished so far, I have big dreams to interview Serena Williams, Simone Biles, Taylor Swift, and Zendaya. I'd love to cover the 2024 Olympics in Paris, too!

I'm also excited to explore more non-sports-related journalism, like more red carpet interviews.

As a sports journalist and broadcaster, my future is only just beginning. I have been able to take negative experiences and use them as fuel to better the world! The passions bullies tried to shrink within me have introduced me to a community of supporters that continue to build me up.

By having this platform, I have met so many amazing people, personally and professionally, who appreciate and connect to my story!

Out of all I have gained from my experiences so far, I realize I must be *myself*. It sounds easy, but it can be hard sometimes. But if you stay true to you and your dreams, no one can tell you who to be.

You can never be *too much* of anything when you're simply being yourself.

About the Author

Pepper Persley is a 12-year-old reporter based in New York and the host of the *Dish with Pepper Podcast*. Since she started her career as a journalist, she has reported for ESPN's MLB's Little League Classic KidsCast and Toy Story Funday Football, and has interviewed some top women athletes such as A'ja Wilson, Sylvia Fowles, Chari Hawkins, Renee Montgomery, Sabrina Ionescu, and Caitlin Clark to name a few. Her work has been featured on *CBS Morning*, *The Jennifer Hudson Show*, *Black Enterprise*, and *Sports Illustrated*.

About the Publisher

Young Authors Publishing is an imprint of Muse Inc. and publishes diverse fiction and nonfiction works written by BIPOC young writers. The publishing house champions narratives that reflect the complexities of our world, and creates space for underrepresented voices to share their own stories on their own terms. Young Authors is on a mission to redefine the literary landscape through diverse stories and writers.

ISBN: 9780998877587

Design by Jenni Oughton.
Illustrations by Jessica Jones.

Young Authors Publishing,
an imprint of Muse Inc.

www.museinc.net